HOW RELEVANT IS EDUCATION
IN AMERICA TODAY?

Kenneth B. Clark
Alex C. Sherriffs

Published by

American Enterprise Institute
for Public Policy Research

Americans are greatly vexed by the troubles besetting their educational institutions. There is ample reason for anxiety. Wholly apart from the difficult, still explosive process of school desegregation, the once tranquil halls of many high schools, colleges, and universities are in a state of unease, some critically so.

Analyzing these problems are two prominent educators, one white and one black, both psychologists, and each the subject of some controversy himself.

Dr. Kenneth B. Clark of New York University, president of the Metropolitan Applied Research Center, Inc., in New York City and the only black member of the New York State Board of Regents, argues that a total reorganization of the educational system is necessary to obtain effective public education. A critical factor in such a reorganization, he says, would be the elimination of present procedures whereby public schools are organized in terms of racial and economic distinctions among students. He believes ghetto children can receive a good education in spite of their environmental disadvantages if teachers are competent enough and work hard enough. In the spring of 1970, Dr. Clark recommended a plan to revitalize the Washington, D. C., school system by offering incentives to teachers based on their pupils' reading progress. The plan was adopted by the Board of Education over the opposition of the teachers' union, and has been causing quite a controversy in the nation's capital ever since.

His debate opponent is Dr. Alex C. Sherriffs, special assistant for education to Governor Ronald Reagan of California.

Formerly, Dr. Sherriffs served as professor of psychology and vice chancellor of student affairs at the University of California, Berkeley, the university where student violence first was spotlighted nationally. He blames irresponsible but influential faculty members for instigating many of the destructive university riots. Blaming the students, he says, is a fiction "born because of its convenience to both the faculty and administration." Too often, he adds, both faculty and university administrators want the public to believe that society is facing a "new breed" of student rather than a power grab by certain elements within some of our faculties.

This book is a record of the Sherriffs-Clark debate on the question, *How Relevant is Education in America Today?* It is one of a series of Rational Debate Seminars sponsored by the American Enterprise Institute for Public Policy Research. In their arguments, both educators cover the academic waterfront, from kindergartens to post-graduate schools. Dr. Clark concentrates on the elementary and secondary systems, while Dr. Sherriffs has more to say about higher education.

Dr. Clark hits hard at "such fetishes" as the neighborhood school. He criticizes the case against busing, and maintains that more children in America are transported to maintain segregated schools than to bring about nonsegregated schools. Besides, millions of Americans, he declares, are transported by bus to rural and consolidated schools without regard to race. Thousands and thousands more are transported for special cooperative educational services set up in many school districts, and many more to attend parochial schools.

In fact, Dr. Clark says, the solution to our pressing social problems depends upon total reorganization of our public schools on a multi-racial, multi-economic basis. "It is my opinion that the problems of social stability, urban and ghetto blight, and the underlying manifestations of cruel racism cannot be solved effectively until such time as the formula can be found for reversing the inefficiencies of the public schools which lower-status minority and white children are required to attend."

Dr. Sherriffs, speaking of higher education, attributes the deterioration of recent years primarily to (1) the effect of permissive parents who have been "poignantly unsure" of how to exercise authority over children actually anxious for guidance, and (2) irresponsible academicians who have lost sight of the ingredients of true education. Focusing on the academicians, he says that never before have faculties been so pampered or so young. With the student population exploding, "the recruiting of faculty became an endeavor competing favorably with the recruiting of football players," he states. As a result, the prevailing majority on many of our campuses are "young Turks" with a strong tendency to regard their expertise in a specific academic area as automatically relating to broad general wisdom. "Probably no profession is more prone to making absolute pronouncements about general matters on which it has no more specific information than the rest of the population than academia," he asserts. "Given these characteristics, and recognizing that the silent majority exists in the faculty as well as in the rest of society, those faculty members, often the younger ones who believe that the world is too complex for the average citizen, or who associate themselves with particular social or political movements, can and have used their genius—and their students—to further their own ends against the best interests of both their more passive colleagues and our society."

Thus, Dr. Sherriffs argues, "a visible segment of the faculty is using the institution for political purposes, is demanding the right to exercise its bias in the classroom, and is milking the prestige of the institution for its own personal goals."

All in all, these two educators zero in on the teaching profession, albeit from different angles. Perhaps Dr. Clark sums up their common concern about teachers: "The teacher's role is probably most important of all . . . there's not going to be any major reform or increased relevance or significant reduction of anxiety in our educational system until the teaching profession . . . develops the techniques,

HOW RELEVANT IS EDUCATION
IN AMERICA TODAY?

*Third in the fourth series of Rational Debate Seminars
sponsored by the American Enterprise Institute
held at
The Madison Hotel
Washington, D.C.*

HOW RELEVANT IS EDUCATION IN AMERICA TODAY?

Alex C. Sherriffs
Kenneth B. Clark

RATIONAL DEBATE SEMINARS

American Enterprise Institute
for Public Policy Research
Washington, D.C.

Library of Congress Catalog Number 70-143719

FOREWORD

From colonial times, Americans have placed a high value on education. And today our faith in its importance and utility remains high.

But we are more and more troubled about the problems besetting our schools and colleges and the directions in which our educational system appears to be moving.

The American Enterprise Institute for Public Policy Research is pleased to present a debate between two distinguished authorities on education. Both are psychologists and both are academicians. What they have to say on the timely question of the relevance of education today — for school children, college students, and adults — merits our attention.

December 1970

William J. Baroody
President
American Enterprise Institute
for Public Policy Research

CONTENTS

FIRST LECTURE

ALEX C. SHERRIFFS

The American citizen has learned to expect much from his educational institutions. This is a high compliment to the performance of these institutions in the past.

Our institutions are expected to carry out high societal purposes:

1. To transmit man's knowledge of man, his make-up, his environment, his culture, his history, his ideas, his dreams, and his failures. Human beings, unlike the monkey, do not need to start from scratch with each successive generation. Man can ensure a continuity of civilization, and his educational institutions are among the most important vehicles for doing so.

2. To stimulate curiosity so as to open doors to learning, to teach students how to ask useful questions, to explore with them ways to seek and to evaluate evidence, and to communicate the significance of bias in the process of reaching conclusions.

3. To develop in the young the basic tools necessary for learning, for communicating, and for effective living.

4. To function within a framework which accepts and values individual and group differences, which shuns as goals indoctrination and homogenization, and which works to pro-

vide for each individual the opportunity to develop to his capacity.

5. To account for the fact that man has always needed to believe in, belong to, or work for something bigger than himself.

6. To provide rich experience with mature teachers and scholars who serve youth as models for adulthood.

The American citizen learned to value highly his educational institutions. They functioned importantly for the society, the culture, and the individual growing student. As a reward to educators and to ensure that their job could be well done, three significant privileges were given: tenure, academic freedom, and unusual independence in hiring and promoting individual faculty members. We entered the 1960s with the academic profession in highest esteem. Its requests were seldom denied; its budget needs grew—and were met substantially, and in good spirit.

Thus it was. But it isn't now. Why?

The answer is, in part, because of the words and behaviors of a highly visible few in the education establishment. The public has no way of knowing how many these few represent, but the public does know that it doesn't hear from those who feel as it does. It is as though the intellectuals have turned against the very functions of education which they had helped educate the public to value and expect. The public reads in the newspaper, hears on the radio, and sees on television professors who only deride and mock the very culture which they were expected to transmit. And the public hears too often from those who are receiving or have just received the best education our society can provide, that this same society must be destroyed.

The public becomes aware, as it reads the college newspapers brought home by its student young, that there are many who are not working to open doors to learning but who, rather, are demanding conformity to their own personal positions and who will shout down, harass, and in some cases even refuse to teach those who express independent thought.

Instead of hearing of the needs for developing the fundamental tools necessary for learning, the public now hears from the campus an emotional call to action by youth—even before they are prepared through rational means to know why or how. Emotions are touted by too many as a legitimate substitute for reason.

Appreciation of individual and group differences—with all the richness that they provide a society—rather than a demand for a homogenizing conformity is characteristic only of a mature democratic society composed of mature citizens. At least, this is what most of us were taught in the past. It is not surprising, then, that the public is now confused, and often shocked, by the demand from intellectuals (of all people) for a one-think foreign policy, one-think sexual codes, simplistic explanations of racial tensions—and the demands of so many of these intellectuals that we be just like them.

The public sees its children being overwhelmed by totally negative attacks on U.S. institutions and officials, on democratic principles, and on campuses. In some quarters, even God is dead. What is left when the cynics, the critics, and the activists are done? Man needs something bigger than himself. The public does not know how few or how many cynics there are, but there is only silence from other educators in rebuttal.

Those who have had delegated to them the important tasks of representing a society and of providing models of adulthood for youth have been most prone to imitating the young, emulating them, and seeking popularity rather than respect.

One cannot say often enough that those who engage in behavior patterns which disillusion the citizens of a democratic society are probably a "small percentage." "Probably," for the voices who speak for democracy are an even smaller percentage. The names of Riesman, Hook, Bettelheim, and Hayakawa are now well known, but mostly because they sing solo parts.

The changes in education have gone along with changes in society as a whole, to be sure. But, education's changes have preceded, rather than followed, society's. The changes have been dramatic, they have been massive, they are for our society quite unprecedented, and they have occurred in a very short period of time. Within an autobiographical frame of reference, I find it sobering.

It is sobering to feel a need to remind audiences of certain fundamentals of human nature, and of the alternate ways that man can live together—in some form of democracy, totalitarianism, or anarchy.

It is equally sobering to need to point out—and not only to youth—that without shared values, attitudes, codes, and some restraints, man is no more than an animal.

We are fortunate to have a society in which we determine our own restraints. In this democratic society, we make our own laws and can change them at will—majority will. We also choose our own leaders and can remove them by majority vote. In short, we determine our own goals within a remarkable system. Perhaps fewer than 1 percent of all human beings have experienced the degree of self-determination that we enjoy. How strange that today we are forced to argue for the survival of that dignity.

Perhaps the basic challenge to our society has always been to balance freedom for the individual with freedom for others, too. The danger is that we will not work together to maintain that delicate balance, but will, as we today become polarized, allow ourselves to be represented only by those who advocate license—or freedom without responsibility—and by those who say we must have no freedom at all.

Democracy is fragile. Even in the best of times, its health requires that the majority participate actively in its processes. When too many "drop out," then those extremists who never could have won in fair competition for the political and social stage may find themselves on that stage alone—and in charge. It is no accident that in his *Republic,* Plato's most pessimistic dialogue was on democracy, and that the one which followed immediately was on despotism.

Who does not feel concern who compares our situation six years ago with our situation today?

Six short years ago in California, for example, higher education had universal respect. But today, we find a public outraged by, and fearful of, those on the campus—for they have organized and launched political and social action from within the people's own educational institutions.

Six years ago, no one dreamed that buildings would be captured, property destroyed, and official files rifled by some of the most educated of our youth.

Six years ago, neither students nor members of the faculty had kidnapped, captured, or held hostage representatives of a democratic society, whether trustee, college president, or dean.

Six years ago, no one dreamed of a bombing on a campus. Recently, there was a 15-month period during which we had nearly 90 campus-related bombings in California alone. By 1969, members of the faculty of the University of Washington found themselves compelled to say in "the Seattle Statement":

> . . . To condone acts of physical violence on the ground that they are mere exercises in freedom of speech is therefore to strike at the very foundations of academic freedom. The use of force and violence for purposes of intimidation is not freedom of speech but its very antithesis. To blur the distinction is to call in question the whole theory of democratic discussion. . . . Arson, assault and battery, the deliberate destruction of scientific and other equipment, the looting of files of research notes and personal papers, the forcible occupation of buildings to obstruct the performance of university functions, the invasion of classrooms and the intimidation of students—these are not forms of speech at all,

they are overt acts, obviously punishable as such. In society at large these are felonies or misdemeanors. In a
university community, they are something more—they
amount to a betrayal of freedom itself.

Six years ago, leaders on our campuses were working to
effect an "open forum policy" so that students could hear
firsthand the widest variety of opinions and attitudes from
visiting speakers, including Communists. Today, on those
same campuses, it is extremely difficult for the moderate, the
responsible liberal, or the conservative to be heard at all.

Six years ago, it would not have occurred to a speaker
that in almost any adult audience there would be a sizable
number whose children were on drugs. Today, a speaker is
uninformed if he does not maintain that assumption.

In six short years, our campuses have moved a long way
—a long way from their original definition and high pur
pose, a long way from their position of public respect and
confidence. How did this happen?

There are, perhaps, as many explanations offered for our
recent societal upheaval as there are observers to it. Each individual will weight heavily those factors which he, because
of bias, training, or life experience, sees of greatest import.
But it has become clear to most of us that our anguish does
not arise from a single cause. In my own analysis, I would
stress at least five aspects which had to be present for our
campus problems to have exploded with such apparent sud-
denness.

First, there had to be a majority of the public who were

silent, confused, and even misinformed about matters as fundamental as the meaning of the behavior of their own children. But also, for the seeds of unrest to have found such fertile soil on the campuses, there had to be highly motivated, hostile, and articulate cliques of irresponsible faculty members on a number of them. These exercised unusual influence because of the immobilization of their generally preoccupied and timid colleagues. It was necessary, in addition, that the campus administrators be generally incapable of coping with irresponsibility and militancy both because of personal factors and because of currently accepted "styles" of administration. It was necessary, too, that extremist groups and individuals, always present in our society, find themselves essentially without competition for the political stage, and thus achieve for themselves success upon success —often to their own great surprise. Finally, there were and are the actions, reactions, counteractions, and counter-reactions that developed from this brew and which spiral the issues and the people into new and increasingly dangerous arenas.

What is the silent majority? Even a casual look reveals some things that are different these days about the citizens of our society—both young and old. There are too many examples of a lack of participation in normal affairs by great numbers of people, and of large numbers failing to support cultural values. Cultural values survive only when the people support them. One need not be a profound student of democracy to understand the implications of the following:

Two hundred classmates observed a bully taunt one of

their number, then knee him in the groin, and finally use his toe repeatedly to remove the boy's eyeball. Not *one* of the 200 cried "Stop," not one tried to get others to help separate the participants, and not one went for help. Ten years ago, it could not have happened. Two hundred classmates at a middle-class school would not have watched as though observing a television screen, and they would not later have explained their behavior as did these 200: "I am not my brother's keeper," or "It was not my fight," or "I didn't want to get involved."

Age is not the explanation, for equally clear were the implications when 38 adults in New York simply watched from their apartment windows as a woman was stabbed to death. Three episodes of stabbing were involved, it all took 35 minutes, and the woman died horribly. Yet not one of the 38 known observers so much as phoned for the police.

The fact that a very small percentage of students votes in student body elections should concern us deeply. So should the voting record of adults in school district elections.

The tiny attendance of students at campus meetings for outside speakers (except for extravagantly controversial ones) is paralleled by the usual nonattendance of most faculty at meetings of their colleagues, and by the nonparticipation of the public at most meetings of college boards of trustees or of local school boards.

Can we say anything about the "silent majority" other than the fact that it is silent?

There has been considerable research about youth. It tells us of current characteristics which partially explain how it is that so many have neither the strength nor the equipment to stand up individually for their convictions. Though better trained intellectually, they are found to be more isolated as individuals and more lonely. Their friendships are shorter in duration and more superficial in nature. David Riesman, author of *The Lonely Crowd,* reports that, during the past ten years, students average fewer friends each year. Thus, they lack the experiences to mature socially and emotionally as rapidly as generations did before.

Researchers also say that more youth show themselves less capable of postponing gratifications, less able to tolerate probabilities and shades of gray, and more demanding of absolutes.

Investigators generally agree that youth, as a group, is having problems with authority. And, as one of these investigators noted, how could it be otherwise when they have had *so very little experience with it?* Too many parents act with permissiveness not resulting from a particular theory of child rearing, but rather as a response to uncertainty and fearfulness about their own roles as adults.

And the communication between the young is poor indeed. An illustration in my own experience says a great deal:

One Saturday afternoon, a rooting section crowd became a mob and behaved in ways far beyond the acceptable. On the following Monday, I asked a class of 400—many of whom had participated—to indicate their attitudes about the debacle. I was a psychologist whose specialization was youth. I asked them to indicate by show of hands, "was the rooting section great," "could it stand a teeny bit of improvement," or "was it poor"? I took the vote on "great" first. A number of hands went up here and there; the other class members were anxiously looking around like the audience at a tennis match during a fast volley. "What was in?" was clearly the question on their minds. Soon, hands were going up around hands that were already up—the "ripple effect." In three minutes, 83 percent were voting "great."

Then I asked for an anonymous paper in which they were to tell me how it was great and how it might be greater. In the secrecy and privacy of those papers, *86 percent* now stated that the rooting section was so bad it should be abolished! And over 50 percent stated, "But what's the use of my feeling this way when I'm the only one?"

I could give all too many examples of this kind of behavior—"in" voting before the group, standing for positions absolutely contrary to personal and private belief.

Let me note here that youth is not without cultural values, but merely is too often unable to express them. A number of factors have worked together to cause our young to be so immobilized in standing for their own feelings, to cause them to be so oriented to what is "in" for the group, to cause them to be incapable of dealing with the minority who now dominate the stage—political and social—the stage that they, the majority, have deserted.

It is worthy of note that:

1. These youngsters are the first children raised by parents who were unsure of their role as parents—even of their rights as parents; the first parents in history who, instead of depending on their feelings, had to "look it up" in a book!

I can give an illustration of the effect:

I gave an anonymous questionnaire to almost 1,000 soph-omores. Two of the questions asked were: "Do you love your parents?" and "Do you respect your parents?" Ninety-three percent checked "yes" to the first question. Only 51 percent checked "yes" to the second question. I called in every eighth student to ask, "Can you help me to understand the differences between 93 percent and 51 percent?" One girl's response covers most of their answers:

Sure, I love my parents. They mean well. But re-spect . . .? When I was in a social club at Berkeley High, I came home one day and told my mother that our club was going to have its overnight party at our house. Mother turned pale. I told her that chaperones were no longer "in," and she turned paler. I hoped she would say, "No, you aren't," and get me out of it, because I didn't have the courage to say no to the others of my own age. If she said "no," I could have blamed her— I thought that's what mothers were for.

Instead, Mother phoned the parents of the other girls and asked what she should do. I listened. She thought it was wrong, but . . . she was afraid I'd be un-popular. She thought it was wrong, but . . . she didn't want me to be "different." She thought it was wrong, but . . . she didn't want my 15-year-old girlfriends to think she was "square." In short, my mother had to dis-cover what her values were— and what mine were to be—by a telephone poll.

Youngsters need adults to be models, to respect, to argue with, and to test. They need a point of view. They need adults who believe in themselves and in something. The young can decide what to become, and what not to become, only by observing real adults. They can learn little that is good from observing Jello—whether in the form of parents, deans of students, teachers, or even clergymen.

2. Also very difficult for youth—and hard on adults, too —is a current cult: the adulation of youth in America. For a child to become an adult, he must, of course, go through what we call "adolescence." This is a period during which the youngster learns where his parents leave off and he begins. He must develop a separateness which enables him to know whether *he* believes something or is merely imitating his parents' belief, whether *he* desires something or has been told by his parents that it is desirable. All of us learn from parents much of what to be like and what not to be like. But, to the adolescent struggling with his dependency needs, it is a matter of "is it me speaking, or am I speaking for them?"

To go through an adolescent separateness—which is often more symbolic than real—the age group members tend to conform to one another, especially in matters which are almost "tribal" in nature: for example, in costume, dance, folk heroes, music, and slanguage. The particular expressions of each adolescent generation have caused parents and teachers alike to shake their heads in dismay. This is as it should be, for it gives the adolescent a kind of independence in action, but without total revolt.

My own parents were ideal during my adolescence. Mother thought my dirty cords meant that I was unclean; she fussed. Both parents believed my swing music to be loud and barbaric, and Mother would often play a little Brahms hoping it would rub off on me. Both were embarrassed by the jitterbug, and they worried that I would never learn to use the King's English. It was ideal. We had our separateness. And it was not necessary for me to take drugs to get a reaction. Later, when I felt that I had discovered "me," I noticed that my parents had "matured" during my psychological absence.

But how is it today? Too often, adults imitate their adolescents. Daughter puts on a mini-skirt, Mother follows suit. Likewise, Father says "cool" to prove he is one of the boys. Both parents learn the Twist and progress to the Watusi.

Adolescence is a time when youngsters should be somewhat separate, but it is also a time when they need to know that there is strength and understanding in the adults. Now, instead—and for the first time in our history—the youngster looks over his shoulder and feels, "My God, here they come again."

By their imitative behavior, adults are saying to youth, "You've got it made," and this is unnerving to the young. To become adult is almost to lose position and status.

And, outside the family, other adult models—many teachers, clergymen, school and college administrators including deans of students—behave in the same imitative ways; and they are representatives of our society and its institutions. They claim expertness as well as adulthood. Yet too many of them prefer peace and popularity to respect. Too many think of the normal expression of authority as a burden, though delegated to them because of the position they hold by a democratic society. A number confuse authority and authoritarian; they reject the former in a manner that smacks of the latter.

3. Progress has brought great good for young and old alike. It also has had its costs. At the turn of the century, most youngsters in growing up had experience with real responsibility and real challenge in relation to the family's work. Over 90 percent of American families were engaged in agriculture. Their children had experience with a variety of adult models doing real work for real purposes and goals. Today, only 7 percent of families produce all of our goods and fiber.

At the turn of the century, there was also ample opportunity for youth in commerce or industry, for work with purpose. It was even necessary to pass child labor laws to keep them in school or at home. Today, if all students wanted such experiences, we would fail them, for, thanks to automation and business know-how, we scarcely have jobs for all heads of household.

In 1900, only 9 percent of 17-year-olds were in school; now there are well over 90 percent.

Today, for many, responsibility and challenge are found only in relation to grade point average. And for many, work is only for one's own pleasures—a transistor, a record player, a sports car.

The cost in judgment, in confidence born of experience,

and in the concept of earning one's way or of work well done when this has not been a meaningful part of life, can be measured only indirectly. Observation tells us that the cost is high.

4. Affluence has contributed to some of our problems. Particularly, affluence leads to a certain arrogance in some youth—an expectation to receive, even though giving little in return. And the comforts and certainties of affluence also result, sadly, in an unsureness that one could succeed if faced with a challenge.

Middle-class youngsters generally are given what they want—sometimes even before they know they want it. Parents too often can't think of reasons to deny them. In giving, parents tend to forget it is more satisfying for youngsters to build, to grow, to contribute, and to participate than simply to be spectators, and recipients of the accomplishments of others.

Affluence, of course, has affected adults as well as children, and it should not be surprising that like spoiled children we also have spoiled adults who simply and irresponsibly take what they want without comprehending what they are doing. It should not be surprising, either, that some middle-class youngsters on the campus take the law into their own hands and interpret our value for freedom as granting them personal license.

5. Another of the forward moves in our society which has produced its own backlash is the explosion in man's knowledge about himself and the world around him. It has been estimated that man has learned more in the past dec-

ade than in his entire previous history and that he will learn more in the next decade than in all that went before.

It is not necessary to dwell on the many good things that have accrued to mankind because of informational advances. But, ironically, the silencing effect of this same knowledge explosion too often goes unmentioned. More and more, individuals are becoming dependent on the so-called "experts" for judgments rather than trusting their own information and wisdom.

6. These days, Americans act as though change, even when it results in instability, is an end in itself. Paradoxically, human beings need a sense of permanence and stability in order to be strong enough to be adventurous, to stand apart from a group, and to take a chance—even though it might result in ridicule or error. Down through the ages, man has sought and profited from identification with a purpose bigger than himself. He has sought immortality, real or symbolic.

When it becomes modern and stylish for members of the clergy to become activists in pursuit of their own personal sociopolitical beliefs, while still identifying themselves with their religion, then many people become less sure of themselves and of their relation to religion, but note!—astrology then becomes the mode! Why else the intense fascination with the zodiac? When representatives of the church attack the very symbols of the church, youth does not become irreligious. Human needs don't disappear, and so youth's search turns to Zen, mystical experience, drugs, and quasi-private cults.

7. Increasingly large, aloof, and distant government has led to a citizenry whose members are becoming less and less involved. It is no wonder they are called "the silent majority."

There are other important factors, too, which have reduced the level of participation—on and off campus. I believe the public's confidence in its schools has been shaken because, in part, the symptoms of the silenced generation have been particularly evident on the campus. The faculties who were assumed by the public to be the leaders and societal representatives among us have shown up very poorly. Further, there are those in the academic community who have chosen to exploit the majority. Those on the campus know it. Those off campus are fast learning it. I think it is important, too, to recognize that the voices from the education establishment are often mouthing only simplistic explanations for campus politicization and turmoil—explanations which the public does not find plausible and which the public sees as self-serving.

It is correctly said that the quality of our educational institutions depends upon their faculties. What has been the quality of faculty behavior in relation to the unrest which has so reduced public confidence?

It requires little thought to conclude that, for a campus to be in trouble, there must be members of the faculty who are both irresponsible and influential. It should be obvious that administrators do not fear students, for students have an average stay on a campus of a little over two years, they are young, relatively inexperienced, and easily influenced. The fiction that our campus problem is simply a student problem is a fiction born because of its convenience to both the faculty and the administration. Too often both would have the public believe that society was facing a "new breed" of student rather than a power grab by certain elements within some of our faculties. It is estimated that, at one time or another, one in every ten students has become involved in campus disorders—but often as a tool for his elders. On this point, David Riesman notes,

> I can think of very few colleges that have had serious student movements without faculty participation. Even though students on both the left and the right like to feel that they are independent of us adults, they are in some ways dependent on adult support. What one finds in some universities is that faculty members have tended to exploit' student protest in pursuit of their own grievances or their own settling of scores with administrators. (*Psychology Today,* October 1969.)

In order to understand how an element of the faculty could behave in ways alien to the whole tradition of the academic community, it is necessary to understand that never before have our faculties been so pampered—nor so young.

Since Sputnik, and until recently, the faculty stood upon a pedestal of public adoration. Education was America's answer to Russia's challenge for the minds of men through scientific achievement. Then with student populations exploding and the production of Ph.Ds several years behind the need, the recruiting of faculty became an endeavor competing favorably with the recruiting of football players. Young scholars who had been singled out because of their brightness during early school years were sought and fought over as graduate students—with fellowships, scholarships, and teaching-assistantships as the bait. As their Ph.Ds were completed, these young scholars were wooed once again by institutions which competed with offers of high salaries, tenure, and, significantly, lower and lower teaching loads.

In the late fifties and early sixties, some of our major institutions added to their faculties as many as a third of these intensely pursued youngsters each year. It was not long before a prevailing majority of the faculties on many of our campuses were "young Turks" who had no investment in the traditions or history of the campus which employed them. Too often, they came in search of a congenial research setting with an aura of prestige, but without a compensating desire to either serve or teach more than necessary. They soon had tenure, and thereafter felt little concern for administrative response to irresponsibility.

It is human, when so sought after and so favored, to accept one's own importance. Humility is not nurtured by such conditions.

There is yet another occupational hazard that we should note here. Ph.Ds know about one specific area as much as, or more than, any other human being—at least for a few months after writing their theses. And Ph.Ds, like other people, because they are human, tend to generalize. There is a strong tendency for them to think that their expertise in a specific area automatically relates to a broad general wisdom. Probably no profession is more prone to making absolute pronouncements about general matters on which it has no more specific information than the rest of the population than academia.

Given these characteristics, and recognizing that the silent majority exists in the faculty as well as in the rest of society, those faculty members, often the younger ones, who believe that the world is too complex for the average citizen, or who associate themselves with particular social or political movements, can and have used their genius—and their students —to further their own ends against the best interests of both their more passive colleagues and our society.

They also have used their influence to recruit new faculty members who share their ideological persuasions. In many institutions, new faculty members are nominated by present staff members, and administrative rejection of such nominations is extremely rare.

A final comment to the layman who has been so patient and who has tried so hard to understand. The academic society is a remarkably closed society. It has its own codes, and demands conformity on many matters. There are few professions that can compete with this one in the exercise of discipline on its members. It also is a profession whose members readily band together, regardless of whatever internal differences, against all outside intervention—even constructive criticism. Already feeling superior to those of less intellectual achievement, criticism from the outside is seen, even by many of the more moderate members, as without justification, wrong, and a dangerous precedent.

We find today a clear illustration of self-fulfilling prophecy. Some faculty groups act almost compulsively to upset the citizens who are the parents of the children on their campuses and the providers of their facilities and livelihoods. All the while, these same educators utter grave predictions of a "right-wing reaction" against the campuses. As some of the faculty escalate their insults, the public becomes ever more ready to lash out—but it is the public as a whole, and not a special element within it, not just parents or the anticipated "right-wing reactionaries."

A third critical element in our campus problems is the campus administrator. Here the difficulty is as fundamental as who he is, and where he comes from. Most administrators were functioning with apparent success only a few years ago. But not today. One must realize that administrators, to be successful for their institutions and for the society whose institutions these are, must be able to wear two hats with relative comfort: They must represent the public interest and the well-being of their students and faculty. This was not difficult when the public interest coincided with faculty goals—unbiased quality education. In those times, the administrator was a coordinator, an interpreter, a fund-raiser, often a mediator within the campus community, and generally a figurehead. Now, the situation is more difficult. The public's basic desires haven't changed, but a visible segment of the faculty is using the institution for political purposes, is demanding the right to exercise its bias in the classroom, and is milking the prestige of the institution for its own personal goals.

Through the administrators, members of the faculty were able to convince a friendly public that it was in the interest of society that they be allowed to pursue the truth wherever it might lead, just so long as they did not tip the scales in the direction of personal bias. The public's acceptance of this was described as "academic freedom." Today, the public is being asked by some to redefine academic freedom in order to grant license to the widest range of behaviors for the faculty and even for students. But a countervoice is absent.

What has happened to the role of an administrator is easy to see. Almost all present administrators have been chosen from the ranks of the faculty, after faculty screening. The wives of these administrators have friends who are, for the most part, faculty wives. The administrator himself was hired originally as a faculty member by faculty members. He depended on them for increases in rank and salary. He, like the faculty member, has been subject to the demands of the academic subculture all of his adult life. It is a rare human being who can wear two hats effectively in an emotionally and ideologically polarized situation, especially when he sees himself as a member of only one of the parties in conflict.

His role is even more difficult because the faculty distrusts administrators, aware of the other hat they might wear. The public tends to distrust academic administrators because it sees them as ignoring their responsibility to the public interest.

A fourth ingredient is made up of the coercive groups which have often been visible leaders of episodes of violence. Tactically and motivationally, the similarities between these groups are greater than their differences. They are alike in that they would never have held the stage if the majority were functioning, if the faculty were united and responsible, and if the administrators had wisdom and courage. They are alike in that they intend to seize power, or to destroy. They advance causes not to achieve them, but to produce conflict. They are, by and large, well organized and disciplined, and apparently have means of communication and travel superior to that of those they attack. Their pattern has been first to analyze friction points on individual campuses, then to seek out support in strategic places on the campus and in the surrounding community. Certain faculty members, clergymen, sympathetic media people, and indigenous radicals or reflex liberals fill the bill. They push constantly, and they push for more than is possible. They wait for a mistake. As soon as it's even slightly credible, they invoke some greater "cause." The issue may have been visitation rights in girls' rooms; it soon becomes an issue of freedom of assembly, or speech, or academic freedom. They simplistically paint the administrators and those of society who would support lawful processes as rigid, authoritarian, and out of step with the times. Usually, they set up the battle plan so they can win either way: for example, if there is capitulation in relation to a sit-in, they control the building and move forward with new demands; if the administration holds firm and eventually calls for outside help, the militants contrive and then point to police brutality. They are willing to nibble, one issue at a time, because each success

ensures a greater likelihood for the next success. This is a
strategy of takeover. It is, in their own words, revolution.

The public watches in fear and anger, for the progress of
the militants has been rapid and far-reaching—far-reaching
enough so that many thousands of parents have youngsters
who have been caught up in the tactics, if not the ideologies.
The public's response becomes less dispassionate with each
passing month.

Some faculty members have begun to voice their concerns,
too. In the January 1970, issue of *Measure,* we read:

. . . Not that we believe that violence has stopped, will
stop, or will be stopped without a hard, protracted
struggle. The wrecked office of the President of the
Massachusetts Institute of Technology is one of the
newer reminders that violence walks in our midst; and
for those Professor Hope-for-the-Bests who think that
red-painted obscenities in the Institute's rugs should be
explained away as mere aberrations of prolonged adolescence, there is the equally reprehensible and hideous
reminder put before us by Princeton's 34-year-old revo-
lutionary sociologist Charles W. Wheatley, who is
quoted in *Time* as saying: "Older faculty are ineduca-
ble when it comes to the revolution, the movement.
They won't be shot, you know; a little island will be
found for them some place."

I think it is vital today to differentiate between three
look-alikes: adolescent rebellion, the American right to dissent, and revolution. They may look alike, but they are not,
and many people who should know better get them confused.

I have described adolescent rebellion as an essential, healthy stage between childhood and adulthood. It can only be destructive if, on the one hand, it is treated with total rigidity, or, and this is more likely these days, it is not resisted at all and thus misses its value for teenagers who must go to more extreme behaviors to achieve an appropriate adult response.

The American right to dissent is worth preserving at any cost. It represents the strength of our society. It is dissent which ensures that there are civil liberties and civil rights, that there is individuality, and that there can be the potential for constructive change.

Revolution is neither growth nor a form of dissent. It is something far different. In this society, it is an effort by a few to thwart the will of the majority and to do so by destroying the democratic system itself.

Finally, there are myths which circulate in society and are supported by too many people of influence who simply parrot them without thinking things through. Some of these myths are given credibility by sincere individuals who simply cannot or do not wish to comprehend what is happening. This all-out attack on our democratic system is a "first" for us, after all.

Though the public has been remarkable in its ability to sense the basic problem, some of the myths that the public believes, or half believes, have served to make people unsure enough of themselves to keep them from responding consistently or appropriately.

I have already talked to the facts which belie several of

the more prevalent fables of our time. For example, the myth that it is primarily the students who are engaged in unrest is both an oversimplification and a distortion.

The myth that we are experiencing a "generation gap" that is nearly a chasm has done great harm. It has caused many people of all ages to become self-conscious in their relationships rather than to be themselves. If one will but listen, youth's dilemma is almost the opposite. Adults have put youth in the role of leader, have tried to remove a gap essential to the process of maturation—that is, adolescence.

Somewhat related is the false belief that students are falling over themselves in their desire to participate in governing the universities. An anonymous faculty member describes it this way:

. . . delusions that trouble will never come and that, having come, it will do no permanent harm are, in fact, children in a large family of sturdy misconceptions. None among them has led to stranger consequences than the supposition that the majority of students are deeply interested in *governing* every aspect and dimension of the schools at which they enroll. Columbia's experience in this respect would be pathetic, if it were not also heroic. Administrators, faculty, and students at Columbia came away from their great ordeal of May and June 1968 persuaded that a university is a community of sorts, that it should be governed by a body of elected representatives, and that these representatives should include elected student representatives empowered to vote. But in October 1968, a well-advertised meeting called at Columbia to air the question of the proposed University Senate was attended by less than 100 persons. In November 1968, the student turnout at elections was the lowest in recent years. According to the *Columbia Forum,* "Only 14 per cent of those eligible in the College (394 students) and 4 per cent of the graduate students (166 students) voted." The faculty Executive Committee leading the drive to place Columbia under the rule of a Senate accommodated to the imagined fact of student interest took these warnings to heart and so conducted its subsequent operations as to *develop* student interest. In the course of creating the very thing they had believed already existed, the Committee distributed 25,000 48-page pamphlets concerning the future Senate. A faculty leader is quoted in the *Forum* as having said: "Someone from the Executive Committee . . . spoke to groups from every student body in every division. I remember one night when there was one member of the Executive Committee on every floor of the dorms, right before the vote." By such means, student participation in the vote to ratify the Senate scheme was raised to 40.9%.

What would have happened, it may be asked, if the Executive Committee had not haunted the dorms and strained the mimeograph machines? The answer appears to have been given this autumn at a neighboring institution, Queens College, in the City University of New York, which has strong claims to being the campus most disrupted in 1969, its administration building

having served as a traffic center and dormitory for student "activists," both white and black, for weeks on end,
with time out for Easter recess. In consequence of its
troubles, Queens conceived an Academic Senate, to be
ratified or rejected by a week-long vote. The vote was
conducted with the help of the Honest Ballot Association. The polls were open from 9 to 9 through five
weekdays and till noon on Saturday. The issue was
thoroughly publicized. Yet out of 24,429 students,
2,724 voted, or about 11%. Asked to comment on the
turnout, a member of the Queens faculty said, for pub-
lication in these columns, "The idea that most of the
students want this change is baloney—if I may call the
sausage by its name."—*Measure,* December 1969

We hear over and over again that "students have real
grievances." The statement is usually followed by another,
"Though, of course, I don't condone their tactics." Involved
here is a half myth, half truth. But those who speak of student grievance usually have been fooled, at least partially,
by the issues put forth by the militants. These issues are not
the real grievances.

It is becoming increasingly clear that students do have
real grievances, for they suffer an unconscionable neglect by
faculty members on many campuses. The meaning of the
ever-lighter teaching load does not escape students. The
office hour so often unmet by the faculty member says something, too. The absentee full professor and the more often
present teaching assistant attest to the same thing. Teaching

students is not, in the minds of many faculty members, the primary purpose of the university or of their careers.

Research and scholarship which bring status in academe have left little time for students. However, there has yet to be a "demonstration" or violence around this issue. It would seem more likely that, feeling frustrated and disappointed after working for years to get to college only to find there an impersonality born of disinterest, these students are more likely to be caught up in somebody else's "demonstration," if only to let off steam in relation to the "system" which has failed them.

For some time, we have listend to a chorus which tells us that in the younger generation there is a "new morality." Usually, we are also told that we should adjust to it. The "new morality" has been preached so effectively that the new generation, as well as the old, believes it to exist. The *College Poll* finds that 75 percent of students believe that most students, whether male or female, engage in sex relations before marriage. In surveys of my own, I have found that senior college women, for example, when asked to estimate the percentage of senior women who have had premarital sexual intercourse also predict on the average that same 75 percent. However, recent studies by Freedman and Halleck, as well as others, indicate that the percentages are in fact between 20 and 22. In the 1950s, Kinsey—and later Ehrmann—reported similar findings. If the data on sexual behavior in the sixties surprise you, then this, itself, is evidence of the effectiveness of a myth.

There are other data on youth which stand in interesting

relation to popular belief. For example, from the *College Poll* we learn that 87 percent of students stated in 1968 that they did not believe violence of any kind is ever justified in bringing about change in the college or university. Eighty percent believed that students who break the law on campus should be arrested and expelled. Seventy-three percent reported believing in God or in a Supreme Being. Eighty percent believed that voluntary ROTC belongs on the campus. Seventy-six percent favored campus participation in defense contracts. And 67 percent voted favorably on the CIA.

It becomes clear that generalizations have been made on the basis of the behavior of student extremists and by the wishful thinking of some emotionally involved observers of the campus scene.

It is important to note, however, that there are some startling differences in the attitudes of the 30 percent of the 17-to-23 age group who are in college as compared with the 70 percent of the same age group who are not. According to the Yankelovich poll for the Columbia Broadcasting System, when asked whether they would welcome *more* emphasis on law and order, 57 percent of college students said yes, while 80 percent of those youths not in college so responded. Twice as many in college indicated they would welcome more sexual freedom—43 percent as compared to 22 percent. While 60 percent of those not in college believed patriotism to be very important, only 35 percent of college youth agreed. Saying that they easily accept the prohibition against marijuana were 48 percent of college students, while 72 percent of noncollege youth so responded. Where we are given data on the parents, we find that youths not in college are quite similar to their parents in those attitudes which relate to our mores. Those in college are less so. It can be said that, though there is generally little evidence of a generation gap, there is considerable evidence of a cultural gap effected by only a few years on the college campus.

As 1969 closed, there were predictions of efforts among the militants to "cool it" for the time being. An election year, a desire to get public support for the 18-year-old vote, and recent effective legal actions against violence were among the reasons. Also, man's growing concern with his environment and with the disastrous effects of drugs on his children will occupy much of his attention.

As we all know, the "cool" was short-lived, and campuses and their surrounding communities are now being subjected to even worse violence than before. And the public is more afraid and more angry than before.

I have taken some time to say that the causes of our present discontent are several and complex. Because time is limited, some aspects have been neglected and exceptions to generalizations sometimes have been ignored.

The public's confidence in higher education is lower today than probably ever before in this country. Many of our institutions have in fact been deflected from their pursuit of society's highest goals.

When we address ourselves to the all-important question, "How do we improve this difficult situation?" our behavior will depend on our understanding of the causes of the symptoms we hope to treat.

To the extent that confusion within the public is a part of our problem, the people should be provided accurate information. Evidence must be substituted for fantasy, facts for myths. The full complexity of the campus crisis must be communicated. We have suffered too long with simplistic interpretations. The majority must be allowed to learn, where this is the case, that it is in fact the majority. It is important that the public see that those who represent them are individuals who are spokesmen for basic educational and societal values. The variety of channels for citizen effectiveness must be made apparent to those who have for too long remained uninvolved in their social institutions. It is ironic that while some groups have developed sophisticated ways to get around or even to injure our democratic system, all too many citizens need a course in Applied Civics 1-A.

To the extent that the representatives of the people have been preoccupied with the activists and have related to their "demands" as a point of departure, it becomes evermore important that educational boards and commissions become effectively accountable to the citizenry.

To the extent that administrators are part of our problem, appointments to such positions should take into account the difficulties of the position for those who are too closely dependent on a constituency at one pole in a societal difference of opinion. Possibilities for finding administrators who are management-oriented and above politics must be improved.

To the extent that elements of the faculty represent an important part of our problem, appropriate administrative support for the many responsible faculty members, a re-evaluation of tenure policies, and a program to ensure a better acceptance of the teaching function are all essential.

Many administrators have been reflexly responsive to the demands of the militant faculty few. If only they would listen to the many—and there are many. On April 23, 1970, we read of a survey of the attitudes of 60,447 university and college faculty members: "More than 80 percent of the respondents held that 'campus demonstrations by militant students are a threat to academic freedom.' More than 76 percent agreed either strongly or with reservations that 'students who disrupt the functioning of a college should be expelled or suspended.' . . . the survey was taken during the 1968-69 academic year."

Coercive groups must be controlled so that they do not interfere with the rights of others. Implementation of relevant legislation and regulations is important, as is the education of students and the citizenry as to the true meaning of the militants' behavior. Policy decisions by campus leaders must not result from coercion. Otherwise, matters become far worse.

Students in general need to be educated as to what present 17-to-23-year-olds are like. They don't know. They must receive appropriate interest and attention from faculty members and administrators. They must see that even those who behave normally will be listened to. They should be used in advisory capacities where they have competence. But they should not find themselves being pandered to. Giving them responsibilities for which they are not ready and in relation to which they cannot represent other students is not a kindness. They know that those who would buy their support are insincere.

Further, institutions should never *require* students to belong to organizations if those organizations are ones which will take positions in their name on political or social affairs. The authority of the state or community must not be used to force a student to support attitudes alien to his own beliefs. In this regard, the present *requirement* on many campuses that students belong to a "student government" and support a so-called "student press" becomes suspect.

These are some of the directions necessary, in my opinion, if there is to be a reduction in the present anxiety about public higher education. As has been made abundantly clear, I believe that the anxiety has real bases and will not disappear as a result of any token solutions. In the months ahead, many constructive steps must be taken both on and off the campus. Neither town nor gown alone can solve our crisis.

The presumably broader question has been raised, "How relevant is education in America today?" Whatever one's answers might have been in normal times as to curriculum, course content, class size, teacher training, student mix, and academic goals, answers today depend upon the prior questions: Will education be free of violence, coercion, and bias, and will it be appropriate to a free society committed to majority decision?

SECOND LECTURE

KENNETH B. CLARK

Probably the most direct approach in seeking an answer to the problem posed by the seminar topic is the quote from one of the most eloquent documents concerned with the social complexities inherent in obtaining effective forms of public education in a democracy, not a document written by educators, significantly enough, but by the Supreme Court. In the historical *Brown* vs. *The Board of Education at Topeka* (347 U.S. 483), the Court stated, on May 17, 1954:

Today, education is perhaps the most important function of state and local governments. Compulsory school attendance laws and the great expenditures for education both demonstrate our recognition of the importance of education to our democratic society. It is required in the performance of our most basic public responsibilities, even service in the armed forces. It is the very foundation of good citizenship. Today it is a principal instrument in awakening the child to cultural values, in preparing him for later professional training, and in helping him to adjust normally to his environment. In these days, it is doubtful that any child may reasonably be expected to succeed in life if he is denied the opportunity of an education.

The rationale and the basic function of democratic education have not been stated more succinctly. And, if these functions were being effectively fulfilled, there could be nothing other than a resounding negative answer to the question posed by those who are responsible for planning this seminar.

In other words, if our public schools were preparing American children for constructive and creative roles in our society—if they were providing them with a "foundation of good citizenship"—then the present widespread anxiety about public education in America would not be justified. Indeed, the gnawing anxiety which demanded that there be a seminar on this topic is almost in itself evidence that all is not well in this most critical area of our society.

Specifically, the evidence is that the anxiety related to the quality and effectiveness of public education in America is more than justified. In fact, flagrant and subtle forms of inefficiency in American public education have reached a most critical, if not catastrophic, stage in at least the following problem areas:

1. The massive inefficiency in the education of lower-income and minority-group children in urban and rural schools.

2. The subtle but critical incompleteness in the alleged effectiveness of public education provided for more privileged white middle-income children in our public schools.

3. The rigidities and resistance to change on the part of those responsible for policy, procedures, and practices in American public schools.

The persistence of these problems more than justifies the present anxiety about public education in America.

MASSIVE INEFFICIENCY IN THE EDUCATION OF MINORITY GROUPS AND LOW-STATUS WHITE CHILDREN

The evidence supporting a contention of criminally ineffi-cient education of the masses of lower-status children in the public schools in America has been documented by a series of major studies within the past ten years and is now over-whelming and undebatable. All American educators—and probably a considerable proportion of the informed public—are now aware of the following disturbing facts:

1. That the average child in the low-status and low-income areas of our cities is markedly retarded in the basic academic subjects of reading and arithmetic.

2. This retardation, which is observed by the third or fourth grades, increases cumulatively through the eighth grade; by high school, these children are unable to compete with more privileged children academically or for those jobs which require minimally adequate academic preparation.

3. A disproportionately high percentage of these students are viewed as disciplinary problems, as "disruptive" in class-room behavior by the time they are in junior high school; their overt restlessness is a prelude to dropping out of school before completing the requirements for an academic high school diploma.

4. Due to a complexity of reasons, many of these young-

sters, in addition to dropping out of academic schooling, are also unprepared for any serious and constructive occupational role in the secondary vocational schools.

This total pattern of failure, inefficiency, academic and vocational retardation is part of the cycle of rejection, despair, and hopelessness in which low-status children are perceived as uneducable, while they, in turn, perceive school personnel and officials as adversaries.

This cycle of educational inefficiency and retardation results in massive wastage of human potential. American public schools, which were conceived and supported as chief instruments in facilitating democracy and social and economic mobility, have become, for these children, not only a formidable force in blocking realistic mobility but, for many of them, a primary source of a dehumanizing and pervasive form of frustration.

It is my opinion that the problems of social stability, urban and ghetto blight, and the underlying manifestations of cruel racism cannot be solved effectively until such time as the formula can be found for reversing the inefficiencies of the public schools which lower-status minority and white children are now required to attend.

Indeed, it might not be possible to reverse this pattern and to obtain effective public education without a total reorganization of our public schools. The critical factor in such reorganization would have to be the elimination of the present procedures whereby public schools are organized in terms of racial and economic distinctions among the students.

Certainly the most important suggestion emerging from the findings of the Coleman Report was that it is possible to raise significantly the academic achievement of lower-status children if they attend the same classes with children from higher-status families.

While this suggestion cannot yet be accepted as an unquestionable fact, it is provocative and does point to the necessity for those who are seriously concerned with the problems of contemporary public education to address themselves seriously to the need to reorganize our public schools on a basis not of the present biracial and economically discriminatory patterns, but on the basis of a multiracial, multi-economic system of school organization.

The difficulties in organizing public schools in democratic rather than in nondemocratic terms are formidable. A welter of historical, dogmatic assumptions, and prejudices that stand in the way must be faced and resolved. Such fetishes as the concept of the sanctity of the "neighborhood school," for example, has been used effectively to divert attention from the need to experiment with more educationally sound approaches to public education.

The recent preoccupation with what appears to be an essentially spurious problem of the transportation of children to achieve more democratically organized schools is an ironic example of the extent to which the prejudices of the past interfere with the educational imperatives of the present and the future.

I refer deliberately to the irony of the anti-busing argument because this particular example of restricted prejudice has recently been articulated by the Vice President of the United States, who used the prestige of his office to propagate the notion that there is something inherently wrong in this approach to effective education—in busing American children to achieve integration.

It is difficult for me to believe that Mr. Agnew and his advisers did not know what a recent study of the Southern Regional Council merely confirmed; namely, that many more children in America are transported to maintain segregated schools than are transported to obtain nonsegregated schools.

It is difficult for me to believe that the Vice President of the United States would have dared to make a public pronouncement on so critical an issue as public education and social stability without knowing of the millions of American children who are transported by bus to rural and consolidated schools without regard to race; and without knowing of the thousands and thousands of children transported for special cooperative educational services set up by a number of school districts; without knowing of the thousands transported to private and parochial schools. In fact, a crucial court case on use of public monies for parochial schools dealt precisely with funds for busing.

In his criticisms of busing for integration, Mr. Agnew and all public and educational officials who share this view must be prepared to argue on precisely the same grounds against *all* forms of busing of children, or else stand accused of a pernicious form of racism.

These many forms of traditional prejudices and restricted

assumptions contribute to the present anxieties in public education since they interfere with the ability to make the types of plans and to implement the plans necessary to increase the effectiveness of public education.

They consciously or unconsciously argue that the present manifestations of educational ineffectiveness, as they are reflected in the academic retardation and general dehumanization of lower-status children in our public schools, are more acceptable than the changes which are necessary to correct them.

Bluntly stated, this is an argument which, in effect, says that this society considers these children expendable.

Such arguments can only be seen as symptoms of a hypocritical democracy and are suggestive of the fact that public education has outlived its usefulness as an instrument of democracy.

Some educators and social scientists do not, however, wish to be openly identified with the more obvious undemocratic explanations of the unwillingness of the society to deal effectively with the problems of public education in America. Some argue that, while it would be desirable to alter policies and practices to increase the academic performance of lower-status children in our public schools, this is not a matter which can be determined by educators; that it is a political matter which must be decided by those with political and economic power.

These individuals argue that it is not the function of the schools, or that those responsible for operating them do not have the power to change the basic patterns and prejudices

of the society. They may supplement this argument by asserting that the schools can at best merely reflect existing values
and practices, since the schools are dependent upon the
existing social and economic system for their own survival.

My argument against this point of view is rather simple—
probably oversimple. If this is true, the value of educational
institutions is disturbingly limited. The affirmative purpose
of education in a democracy is to guard, to strengthen, to
perpetuate values—even in the face of the society's inability
at any particular moment in history to understand or act in
terms of the importance of these values.

Educational institutions, from the elementary schools
through our most prestigious graduate and professional
schools, must have as their primary function to serve as custodians of the cherished human and democratic values of a
civilized society. If this is not their primary function, there
is grave reason for the most devastating forms of anxiety
concerning the state of public education in America today,
an anxiety merely symptomatic of the profound concern
which all thinking human beings must now have in regard
to the stability of the society as a whole.

Another group of social scientists argues—from my
perspective, unconvincingly—that the chronic academic retardation of lower-status children in our schools cannot be
understood as reflecting any general inefficiency in the public
schools, but as reflecting larger problems of social and environmental deprivation and pathology which make it impossible for these children to learn, no matter how effective and
compassionate their teachers might be.

Indeed, these educators and social theorists who offer as an explanation the theory of cultural deprivation often do so with compassion and with an environmentalistic liberalism which is difficult to reject on ideological or even human terms. They demonstrate their compassion by asserting explicitly or implicitly that the problem of academic retardation in these children can only be resolved by major social changes which remove persistent racism and economic and other forms of inequities from our society.

I have a major disagreement with those who assert that the anxieties about public education in America are not to be understood in terms of specific problems of the schools and who insist that these educational problems are to be understood in terms of the problems which the students bring to the schools.

This might be true, but the evidence is not yet convincing. This approach violates the law of parsimony which insists that simpler explanations must be examined and ruled out on the basis of evidence before more complex or abstract explanations are accepted. The proponents of the cultural deprivation theory have not eliminated the simpler explanation of effectiveness of classroom teaching in schools attended by minority-group and lower-status children; and they have not ruled out the explanation in terms of the extent to which racial and economic determinants of school organization, morale, supervision, and accountability affect directly the academic performance of the children attending lower-status schools.

In passing, one must now briefly address oneself to the

fact that there has been a resurgence of explanations of the academic retardation of lower-status children based on theories of inherent racial inferiority.

Professor Jensen has brought this matter of racial genetic theories back into "respectability." In doing so, he has attempted to reduce the basis for anxiety concerning quality and effectiveness of our public education by transferring the anxiety into the presently uncontrollable area of genetic transmission of academic ability.

If Professor Jensen is correct, there need be no educational anxiety about the quality of our public schools in preparing masses of minority-group youngsters for a constructive role in our society; there need only be a biological anxiety. Those of us who are concerned with reducing the number of educational casualties would have to address ourselves to techniques for biological controls rather than to techniques of educational controls.

It is my considered judgment that Professor Jensen has no more basis in evidence for his contention that the academic retardation of minority-group children is genetically determined than he would have evidence in support of a contention that the academic retardation of lower-status white children is genetically determined.

In the light of this absence of evidence, those of us who are concerned with the stability of our society and with increasing the effectiveness of democratic public education, and thereby, with reducing realistically our anxieties concerning public education, must continue to address ourselves to the concrete matters of public school reorganization, teacher training, accountability within the schools and the classrooms, and those human, moral, and ethical considerations which make for effective public education in a democracy.

INADEQUACIES OF PUBLIC EDUCATION FOR PRIVILEGED WHITE CHILDREN

Almost invariably, the discussions of the inadequacies of those public schools reserved for minority-group students seem to suggest that the quality of education provided for more privileged white students is ideal, and that these students are provided with the type of public education which will equip them to cope effectively with the complex demands of the present and the future world.

One of the poignant findings resulting from my interviews, conducted in preparation for my testimony for the school desegregation cases in 1951, was the discovery that the Negro children attending the segregated schools in Clarendon County, South Carolina, and Prince Edward County, Virginia, invariably believed that the white schools in their communities offered excellent education to their own white students. These Negro children believed that the teachers in the white schools were superior and that all facilities, supplies, and the general educational tone in these schools, which they perceived only from a distance, were beyond question superior to anything which they experienced in their own Negro schools.

These Negro students believed that it was impossible for

them to compete academically with the children attending the white schools because of the obvious inequality of their own schools. The tragic fact is that this perspective was more often than not—if not always—supported by the reality.

An interesting footnote to this point was found when I interviewed the Negro students who were involved in the desegregation of Central High School in Little Rock after they had attended the Central High School for a few months. When I asked these students what was the most positive thing they had learned that seemed to justify all of the turbulence they had endured, one of them replied, "I learned that there are as many dumb white students as there are dumb Negro students. I really didn't know that before."

This broadening of perspective seemed to me at that time an unexpected dividend in the struggle for public school desegregation.

Given the fact that schools attended by privileged white students are almost always obviously superior—or perceived as being superior—to the schools attended by minority-group children, including superiority in the quality of teaching, and in the ancillary educational services and facilities, it is not surprising that academic performance measured by standardized tests and other indices of academic superiority is, on the average, consistently superior in privileged white schools to the performance of lower-status children in segregated and lower-status schools.

It is difficult to argue persuasively that the education provided for these privileged middle-class white children is inadequate and could in any way serve as a basis for the current anxiety about the overall quality of public education in America. It is my considered judgment, however, that public education in these privileged schools is indeed a most important basis for anxiety and serious concern.

If one were to define the function of education exclusively in terms of apparent academic success, reflected in passing existing standardized tests in reading and arithmetic and in terms of the student's ability to communicate orally and in writing with a fair degree of coherence, then it would seem that the public schools attended by middle-class children are adequate. These children do, in fact, on the average, function at or above the norms of their grades, while lower-status children on the average function generally below the norms for their grades. In upper middle-class suburban public schools and in specialized urban high schools most, if not all, of the privileged white children are trained to make college examination entrance scores which are high enough to assure admittance to a prestigious or an acceptable college.

The social class competitive needs of the parents of these children are supported by the schools in these limited educational goals for their children, and the success and effectiveness of the school are defined in terms of the extent to which these needs of the parents are met. When these goals are not met, the parents generally exercise their power to remove the educational officials and other personnel who are seen as having failed their children.

In short, "good education" for privileged middle-class children and their families is defined in terms of successful

academic competition as measured by the simplistic standards of high scores on multiple choice examinations.

This single-dimensional concept of education appears to
be self-perpetuating. The significant deficiency in the education of these children appears to this observer to be found
in the fact that high academic performance is obtained at
the expense of any attempt to include, as an integral part of
the educational process, the important ingredients of social
sensitivity, moral responsibility, empathy, kindness, and an
awareness that superior intelligence and academic ability impose upon individuals obligations for social responsibility.

This moral retardation which parallels the academic retardation imposed upon lower-status children—this fundamental educational deficiency—seems to have its roots in the
following generally and uncritically accepted processes
which dominate the education of privileged children:

1. Education from the early primary grades is posed in
competitive and anxiety-producing terms. These children are
required to impress their teachers by outdoing and at times
humiliating their classmates. Given this approach, the child
learns from the earliest grades that intelligence and academic achievement are devices to obtain superior status and
economic and social advantages over others.

2. Under these conditions and under the guise of efficiency, children are evaluated solely in terms of educational
potentials and competence, in terms of IQ scores and
achievement scores which necessarily reduce the total complexity that is the individual to a single index of worth.

3. It would follow from the above that more often than not—when academic success is defined in terms of competitiveness—personal anxiety and the reduction of the awesome wonder of the individual to a score would contribute to an inner sense of emptiness, of conflict, and random or specific rebellion.

This type of education, generally provided in isolated, racially homogeneous, hothouse types of schools, fails to provide their students with moral guidelines essential for the effective, creative, and adaptive use of superior intelligence and academic competence.

The rebellion of a critical minority of privileged white students cannot be disregarded as an insignificant social phenomenon which will pass with time; these students cannot be repressed or contained by primitive force and violence. Their anguished cries and insistence upon moral substance and social meaning for their lives cannot be answered by calling them "bums" or by responding to the tragedies which their quest for ethical significance sometimes precipitates by resorting to the pious clichés of concern with "law and order" from them while taunting them with flagrant examples of official lawlessness.

The predicament of these students must be understood in terms of the fact that our social system, and specifically our educational system dominated by and organized in terms of social injustices and cruelties, have left them morally rudderless. These young people are the tragic symptoms of the facts that justify anxiety about our public education. They are seeking to escape a sense of personal guilt. They are seeking to avoid the intolerable problems of identity inherent in their dawning awareness of moral and ethical emptiness.

For some presently unexplained reason, this relatively small percentage of young people is no longer able to accommodate to the functional hypocrisies of the larger society. They are rebelling against their parents, their teachers, their ministers, and they are demanding that their schools and their campuses—indeed, the society as a whole—meet the fundamental human need of ethical substance.

So far, our public schools and our colleges, with few exceptions, have failed them. This failure must be corrected, and immediately, if our society is to survive as a civilized and democratic system.

The schools must be organized as a nonracial system in terms of a racial and economic mix as an affirmative educational requirement. The nature of the school must be perceived as part of the educational environment; ethnic and economic differences must be seen as assets not only to lower-status children whose motivation and achievement will be increased, but also to higher-status, more privileged middle-class white children who have an imperative need to cope with and empathize with others who are different. It will increase, in these children, knowledge of the varieties of human beings, contribute to their poise and social sensitivity, and make them more effective human beings.

Specifically, we must build into the educational program specific designs to meet both the academic and the moral needs of children. Neither can be left to chance. Teachers must be prepared for both of these functions through teacher training courses, through serious implementation of in-service training programs developed to prepare existing teachers. A system of accountability must be developed to supervise the reinforcement of the skills of teachers in dealing with these dual responsibilities. Methods must be designed to regulate, regularly and periodically, the effectiveness of both the academic and the moral components of education. Beyond this, serious techniques must be developed for involving parents of all of these children in the common goals of democratic public education.

I believe that this is possible if we understand that it is imperative. It is critical for all American children that the schools be reorganized to meet these needs. Schools must be freed of restrictive clichés and a massive educational organization must be devised. This is the only way we are going to save our children. They cannot be saved by military adventures throughout the world, but only by our reinforcing the constructive, positive potentials of all our children.

REBUTTALS

KENNETH B. CLARK

First let me say that in reading Dr. Sherriffs' paper, my basic reaction was that I thought it was a most thoughtful and wise presentation of an essentially conservative point of view, and I use the term "conservative" in its nonpolitical or nonideological sense—namely, conservative in seeking to conserve some of the important even though subtle and somewhat elusive values which some of us believe to be essential to the maintenance of civilization.

I must also say, Dr. Sherriffs, that I too, not as a psychologist but as a person whom psychologists study, was in all honesty having my expectations influenced by your designation as the special assistant — (laughter) — to the governor of the great state of California and did in fact approach your paper expecting more Reaganisms than were found there.

The thing that fascinated me about your paper, though, was that you were highlighting some extremely important moral problems and dilemmas that must concern the custodians of civilization, whether they be in the halls of academe or in the churches or in the area of art, etc. You raise these questions. You certainly presented your ideas about their cause.

I share a number of your concerns. Certainly I share the

concern of the extent and the meaning by which individuals who believe themselves to be morally right, almost to the point of dogmatism, assert the right to intimidate others, to coerce others, to prevent others from speaking—or who believe that any method which they choose to use would be justified by their moral certainty.

I, too, have found it necessary to address myself publicly to the fact that an institution of higher education has the obligation to communicate clearly and certainly to students and faculty what the specific functions and purposes of higher educational institutions are. And certainly mindless, irrational violence, or stagnant conformity seems to me to be inimical to what these institutions' role must be in our society.

Here it would seem to me that no rational man could argue that the methods of irrationality and violence, if they have a place anywhere — and I seriously doubt that they should have a place anywhere — have a place in colleges and universities.

I share your concern that, for some peculiar set of reasons, administrators and some faculty members have not been clear enough about this and therefore have defaulted in their responsibility.

But I find myself going beyond your clear statement of these important problems and doing something which I kept hoping that you would do for me—namely, to analyze some of the reasons for the problems. I think you made an excellent inventory of very important problems in higher education: the nonrational, violent conformity; the default on the part of the adults, faculty members, administrators, parents; the poignant story about the young girl who was looking to her mother to provide the restraints and didn't find them, and therefore differentiated between love and respect. These to me are very real and very important problems.

Where I felt let down by your paper was that you did not go the next step and tell me why this happened.

I will now tell you why I think these things happen, with full awareness that this is a reflection of my bias. I think, Dr. Sherriffs, that the things you described in your paper happened because these young people have been let down by a society that is really hypocritical in its morality, and the adults are unable to give guidance because they have been caught. While it is true that the confrontation may have come out of an atmosphere of permissiveness, the substance of the confrontation is real. What we have now discovered, in the sense of bringing it into our consciousness within the past decade or so, is that the verbalization of morality in the society has not been backed up by the substance. And the young people are exploiting that fact. They are putting professors and administrators and church leaders and parents on the spot, sometimes randomly and irrationally and destructively. And they are daring us to assert values, again verbally, when they can demonstrate that functionally we have violated those values. All this is related to Vietnam and Cambodia and racism, because these are now highly specific manifestations that we have gotten away in the past with moral duplicity.

What really terrifies me is the evidence on the part of

many of the young that they would seem to settle for total irrationality and total immorality rather than settle for moral duplicity. I think that's wrong. I will take my chances with duplicity, trying to turn duplicity into substance. When I have a chance to talk with young people, I will say—I'll try not to be defensive—"Yes, all right, you're right, you're right, you're right. BUT the repudiation of all moral guidelines does not offer anything for the preservation of civilization, and it's easier to repudiate than to try to find moral methods by which to get moral substance and to escape moral hypocrisy."

I think this is what the President and the Vice President of the United States and some governors don't quite understand. They act and speak as if it is possible to impose the moral words on young people now despite the flagrant evidence that immoral acts vitiate any appeal. Now, I will agree that this is true only for a minority of the young people. But the last point I will make, Dr. Sherriffs—by no means a refutation as much as it is an elaboration of your paper—is this: You cite statistics indicating that 80 percent of the young people are still accommodating to the uncritical and accepted moral words of our society. And this is unquestionably true. But what fascinated me about your summary was that it was violating a very important point in your paper, namely, your point against conformity.

You made the very telling observation that one of the disturbing things today is that the young people—in your class, for example—looked around to see how the others were going to answer before they answered. I think all you were doing in giving those statistics—which allegedly support the contention that the majority of people are still functioning in terms of moral values—was telling me that the majority of people are still willing to conform to verbal morality. But if you will test those same people to see what their actions are, you will find that they are racist people, that they are people who will say one thing about sex and behave another way about sex, as Kinsey indicated.

It may be that the revolution, in the constructive sense, that we are now embarked upon—and in public education it involves the elementary, secondary, and higher educational levels—is a very serious revolution. It may have to go through some really terrifying stages in order to decide whether we are going to try to continue to play the Russian roulette of moral hypocrisy—namely, verbalization of morality without substantive support of it—or whether we are going to have to suffer the kinds of pain necessary to get to a more substantive form of ethical and moral basis which, I hope, will save not only the youngsters who seem sometimes not to want to be saved but also that majority of youngsters who are stagnant conformists.

ALEX C. SHERRIFFS

You tempted me to rebut the rebuttal before I rebut your paper, Dr. Clark.

I think there are some of the most beautiful descriptions of what education is supposed to be about in that paper. I particularly commend the quotations in it. I think they are excellent statements of what society has a right to expect.

But you describe the values that should go along with aca-demic content as though they were nonexistent in present education. I'm not as much a pessimist as perhaps I've sounded to you, for I find that these values are much more present than absent in teachers—I'm not totally despairing!

On most of the points you make I would concur. I feel that education is generally falling short of what it should be. I think it is falling short more in some schools than in others. I think it is falling short not only because man is fallible, but for other reasons that we can analyze and understand.

I think that the concept of racism as *THE* reason rather than *a* reason bothers me a little because I think there can come a time when we can create the problem if we stick to it as an absolute and if we do not allow it to get well, even when things are being worked out.

I think there are other things that have to be brought in,

too. For example, consider vocational education or technical and vocational education, as we now call it (in much the same way we changed the label from janitor to custodian so it would have more appeal and not be "lower class"). Teachers of vocational education, on the average, feel they are second-class citizens. On the average, they are treated by their fellow teachers as though they are some kind of second-class citizens. And it's got nothing to do with their color. It's got to do with what they're teaching. It is no surprise, therefore, that students who go into vocational classes sense the fact they're going into something second class, even though one's contribution to society can be argued to be important through the skills learned there, and by the choices one can make through this route. This is, it seems to me, a hang up that our society has to cope with, and soon. And it has something to do with whether people who have felt, and have in fact been subject to, discrimination can accept technical and vocational educational routes to their own self-sufficiency. Somehow we are going to have to do something about that. And we are trying hard.

I think the need to work with families, as well as with the youngster in the school, is significant. The family without a library or even without a book is too often a family that doesn't show excitement about what the youngster is learning in school. They fail to give that youngster the feelings of reward, the attention for what he brings home from school. Moreover the youngsters in the neighborhood are all too likely to pick on him for using a multisyllabic word that he has learned, as though he is one-upping them.

There are programs, as we know—innovative, we call them these days—which try to include the family and which try to cope with some of today's dilemmas. I think such objectives are in the picture as much as some inherent racism.

Also some reactive behavior has developed because we have moved rather dramatically, I would suggest, in a very few years. Our movement was way overdue, tragic in its slowness to start, but we have moved from a caste society toward a class society, which means that for many among our minorities the barriers are more permeable for personal growth. As psychologists, we know that when the barriers are fixed, there are certain kinds of anxieties that don't find expression, and certain kinds of aggression that don't occur —but that do occur when *moving* from that caste condition to a class condition.

And I think that the teacher in a junior high school who said to a youngster in the classroom, "*Your* problems are because of *her*" (pointing to a youngster of a different race) does not help people understand one another. When human beings move from a system where they cannot get through barriers to a system where they can, there is jealousy on the part of those who were over on the other side first, as well as anxiety for those getting through the barriers.

I think that our educators have, in part, sold our youngsters short in their ability to understand—an ability they can attain if they are provided the information with which to understand.

I believe that your paper is valuable, Dr. Clark. I read a number of your other papers because I didn't have the

stereotypes of you that you say you had of me. (Laughter.)
So I had to read papers of yours to develop some, and I
found you an eminently knowledgeable, reasonable, decent
human being. (Laughter.) And today I find that that's what
you are in fact.

Now that I've said that, I want to defend myself.

In my own quaint way, in my paper, I thought I was giving the explanation and not the description. I think when I
talk about the effects of my field and yours, of psychology,
on adults who are no longer sure that they can rely on their
heads (we used to call it common sense) and on their hearts
to relate to their own children——

DR. CLARK: Can I interrupt on this?

DR. SHERRIFFS: Sure.

DR. CLARK: Because I think that's true. That's the point
you make, but I then ask: Why? Because certainly adults
now are not less intelligent than our parents were. But
they're less morally sure, I think.

DR. SHERRIFFS: Oh, definitely. But I think the "why" is
the same as the reason people seek you or me out at a cock-
tail party and ask questions about what their dreams mean:
that is, psychology is impressive to other people.

Psychology pretends to have answers and people are, by
and large, not all that secure. When experts in some field,
say, "We know the answers, you should buy our books,"
and when we have best sellers not only in books and paper-
backs but also in magazines, then being overawed by this, as
many persons are, represents human nature, not "hypocrisy."

I think that the knowledge explosion causes people to be

less sure of themselves and to turn too quickly to experts. When I find even my colleagues in the academic world actually quoting Teller and Pauling as the excuse for their position on nuclear testing, and being satisfied to go no further, I think we are seeing a cost of what it is to think that there is too *much* to know. We seek an expert rather than trust our own information. When we do that for value judgments, it is serious, and it also makes us less useful models for our children.

I think that change has become a "fetish," to use a word which you used in your paper, Dr. Clark—change for its own sake, not just change to solve problems. Change of this nature is very unsettling. I'm for change, conservative or not, but I'm not for change just for kicks. When people don't know where anything is going, they become immobilized or lash out, rather than pulling together their resources, as we're doing here in rational debate.

There are a lot of variables that I mentioned in my paper and which I do see as explanatory.

Now, with reference to the private versus the public posture and then reaction to conformity, I would say just the opposite of what you do. First, I'd like to say that conformity is not all bad. "Thou shalt not kill" is a value I hope we conform to without great loss. I hope that going down a freeway on the right side is a conformity that we can afford.

So we should ask, how much conformity? And, do you lose your individuality in conforming?

The example I gave, and other examples I know, suggest that when you give anonymous questionnaires or when you ask anonymous open-ended questions, you get highly "moral" answers. You can get an answer by a public show of hands these days which may be moral or immoral; it is almost irrelevant. It depends all too often on what the voters *think* the group feels.

The example I used that you referred to, Dr. Clark, was the situation in a classroom where students were asked to vote on the behavior of a crowd which became an ugly mob. When the class was asked to vote on whether the behavior had been great, whether it could have stood some improvement or whether it was poor, 500 of the top $12\frac{1}{2}$ percent, gradewise, of high school graduates looked around—like the audience at a tennis match during a fast volley—to see what was "in," and raised their hands accordingly.

Eighty-three percent of them voted that it was great to throw bottles in the faces of girls, to urinate on the lawns of girls' living groups after the game was over, and so forth. They voted "great" 83 percent.

But in the secrecy and privacy of a poll which was anonymous, those same students said it was foul. It wasn't that they were moral in conformance. Quite the contrary. Their public conformity to what they believed to be "in" represents a sick kind of conformity. They may do what's "in," regardless of what they think.

Of course this is also true of many adults. Whether this is hypocrisy, or whether it is a fear that one will not be accepted when one doesn't have enough inner strength, is the question. Riesman has talked a great deal about this.

I think the word hypocrisy is emotionally loaded. It attributes things that are not necessarily there. I feel very sorry for the parent who has to phone the other parent to find out what she should do, but I don't think she's a hypocrite. I think she needs my therapeutic couch. Unfortunately, too many parents do. So I have more than a little unease about the word hypocrisy. When we use it, we start with our own frame of reference.

I hope you were not saying, Dr. Clark, that we can escape hypocrisy by revolution or that revolution will cleanse us or help us find our moral values. I've never known of a revolution yet that hasn't led to more recriminations, more vindictiveness, more double standards and, in a very fundamental sense, more hyprocrisy.

DISCUSSION

ELEANOR MALMBORG, American Association of University Women: Dr. Clark, given the resistance to change, what, if any, promising avenues do you see for dealing with the two major problems that you have discussed: the poor minority-group student in the schools and the affluent suburban student?

DR. CLARK: First, the courts, the federal judiciary, have emerged as the most significant and powerful force in support of fundamental democratic values in our society, more so than churches and, disturbingly for me, more so than educational institutions. It is fascinating that the basic educational and moral issues which the court addressed itself to in these decisions were issues, Dr. Sherriffs, which we and our colleagues, if we had addressed ourselves to them, might have helped a lot of these young people to deal more constructively with their unrest.

So I would put as number one the power and force of the federal judiciary as an instrument in articulating the importance of these values, even though they don't have armies. It was one of our Presidents who said, you know, that the Supreme Court has made a decision; now let it enforce it.

Interestingly enough, the Supreme Court doesn't have the power or the federal courts don't have the power to enforce.

But they certainly have the power to articulate over and over again, to drum in, and there is something about repetition which begins to have some kind of effect, either positive or negative.

The second force, as I see it, is a rather paradoxical, ironic one. It is the critical, small proportion of young white people who are, in a rather Genet-like manner, putting themselves in the place of Negroes, imitating Negroes, demanding that this society treat them as if they were Negroes, showing their feelings by the rejection of middle-class styles of dress, speech, and values, getting themselves tied into the drug and other kinds of self-destructive culture.

I say that this is paradoxically a positive force because in an essentially racist society it may very well be that the society that can accept expendability and self-destruction in rejected minority-group youngsters may have to have second thoughts in seeing this process spread to suburbanite, affluent youngsters.

It is my contention that our society will not be able to deal with this problem—even though it still affects only a minority of young people, including whites involved in alienation and self-destruction—without addressing itself to the kinds of basic changes which will be essential to save all other youngsters.

Now, as a psychologist again, I must- say that I don't believe that many of these youngsters are conscious of what they're doing. Many of them may have rejected the rational or sub-rational analytic process enough not to be doing this in conscious, rational thoughts.

Certainly, suburbia and colleges will have to address themselves to problems of drugs among their middle-class white youngsters, will have to address themselves to problems of moral and rational dropouts among these youngsters and, in doing so, may have to reorganize the whole educational system that will deal with these problems at their root.

MISS MALMBORG: Could I just add—just to make the question more difficult—that I have read the National Education Association Report of the Mississippi Task Force Investigation. I found it terribly depressing, particularly because of the treatment by professional people of other professional people.

DR. CLARK: There is a possibility that we have gotten to the point where we consider everybody sort of expendable now. But if that's true, then we're wasting time in rational debate and should spend our time observing the process of irrational deterioration, which could be fascinating in itself.

JOHANN BENSON, Legislative Reference Service, Library of Congress: I would like to address my remarks to Dr. Sherriffs. Dr. Clark could comment upon them afterwards perhaps.

You outline a number of reasons for the deterioration of our youth, and they are quite interesting.

You say, for example, that this is the first generation of parents in history who have had to look it up in the booktype of philosophy, and then you go on from there to mention the adulation of youth and the glut of wealth and the idea of progress and the accumulation of knowledge. I want to address my question towards the idea of cure which you said you might comment upon afterwards.

One of Dr. Clark's comments dealt with the emphasis put upon the college board scores. Perhaps this has something to do with the cultural problems of Negro people in trying to measure up to other standards.

But my mind goes back to a quotation by Alfred North Whitehead, who observed—in the 1930s perhaps—that what America was losing was its vision of greatness. This goes back to the idea of models, which I think both of you addressed yourselves to—the idea that we focus on intelligence and not so much on character anymore.

There's an enormous difference there, I think, which deifies the mind but not how it's used.

I also want to get the idea of a model for a state, such as the one set forth in a book by J. H. Plumb. I have forgotten its title, but the book commented upon the kind of situation we are in today, contrasting Western society with communism and how communism was a goal-oriented society. The Communists were shooting for something which was kind of marvelous perhaps, and we think never attainable, but still their society had a direction, a focus, and a kind of model that they could attain.

I wondered if you could comment upon this general view of models for action, models for character, models for society and, if possible, would you comment upon how you see the cure?

DR. SHERRIFFS: There are many subtle things, as you

are suggesting. Some of them are overwhelming. Part of the modeling that goes on for the young and for the old, too, is from heroes. Let's not throw out assassination as among the things that are disturbing us. A number of people identified with John Kennedy, for instance, and he died; and they identified with Martin Luther King, and he died; and they identified with Robert Kennedy, and he died. Three rather important models, heroes, were wiped out like that (snapping fingers).

You know, when a person loses a mate, he may be afraid to care too much about somebody for quite a while; when you lose a hero you're often afraid to trust too much for quite a while, too.

I don't know how anybody can measure how much Spock has affected us—I don't mean the political entity but rather dependence on a book instead of on one's head and heart. Youngsters can read a parent's emotions beautifully. A baby will cry if the mother's afraid, without a word spoken, and if the child gets cues that the mother or father feels one way about something, but does something else, then what's for real? That's pretty fundamental.

The loss of heroes is something. The immobilization of people who look to polls to decide where they stand is something. Running for election on the basis of "psyching-out" the public, instead of standing on what you believe, is something.

There are so many of these things and you can't—I can't, God knows, and I don't think you can either—say it's one pound of this and two pounds of that.

When the immature and the young discover they are in many senses the leaders of adults, they become confused. It may be because of fear by the adult; it may be because the adult is caught in a youth cult and wishes to live forever, and dresses like the young, and talks like them; it may be this sellout for popularity rather than respect by adults. You must consider, too, that stable influences are important when you are young. If you get into trouble in adolescence, trying to find out who you are—where the old man leaves off— you need strength at home. When the elders at home are imitating you instead of being themselves, it almost prevents your growth.

If I were to set up the ideal experiment on how to keep youth from growing up, it would be a replica of what we are in, and this is pretty sad. I know all the rational arguments, and so do you, for a clergyman going to the bar dressed like the kids, saying God is dead and so forth. But when he does it, still carrying the label of religion, still saying, "I stand for theology and I'm still the route to afterlife" and so forth, it does something not very funny to people, and not very good.

And lots of people are exploiting their establishment connections these days to push their own personal biases, with a strange lack of ethics. There are those who are using society's institutions—such as a university—to promote their political ends. They are even using, for example, compulsory student government fees to advance the cause of those of just one persuasion. Whatever the cause, this is immoral behavior; it's just that simple. And yet it's done again and again.

So where are the institutions? If I'm any kind of conservative, I'm an institutional conservative. I think man needs institutions. He needs to believe in something bigger than himself. He needs those horizons you're talking about or he becomes at best a pain in the neck.

And those horizons have been very much undermined. Even working for the underdog gets confused. I'm sure some of you know what Steinbeck said when he was given the Nobel Prize for literature. One of the reporters asked him, "How is it, John, that you received this award for the sensitive, feeling portrayal that you gave us in *Mice and Men, Cannery Row, Grapes of Wrath,* and now you are writing *Travels with Charley.* How come?"

And Steinbeck said, "Son, I can't figure out who the underdog is anymore."

I know I have not quite the pessimism that perhaps others have about the route we're going on race relations and about achieving respect for one another regardless of differences.

There have been some very rough times between races in the last few years, but, out West at least, they haven't shaken people's fundamental belief in individuals of the other races. It's quite remarkable how little scapegoating there is, how little attaching a stigma to a group, black or white, because of the behavior of the few.

It is to me most reassuring to see that even after a terrible interracial episode, there isn't an effort to get even with people of the same color as the offender. So I think we've gone beyond some critical point, thank God.

JOHN KENNY, consulting engineer: My field is water management but of late it's pollution control; it's the thing to do. The only difficulty is that with the youth movement coming into it, the youths have equated environment and pollution and they are not equatable. The environment covers everything, but when they come down to it, it's the symptom of pollution that they see, and it's only what they can see, smell, or taste that bothers them.

I participated in seven university teach-ins. I was in on the summary of the polarization at Temple and my pitch to that group there was pretty much along the lines of what I'm hearing here in part. My question was: What was the purpose for the university? Was there a worthy purpose for its continuance?

If there is a difference between man and the other animals, it's the gray cells. But, if man doesn't use them, where are we? We're back to the computers and the kids that are memorizing, we're not thinking.

As far as I'm concerned, there are more confused adult professors than there are confused students. They're in there doing something but with no real purpose in life.

On the pollution bit, we now have three groups involved. We have the politicians who hope to make some hay. We have the faculty members who would like to have a research area to exploit. And then we have the youth who are looking for a cause. They're sincere, they're dedicated, they're concerned.

But once they begin to get facts from both sides and begin to think, we get into another picture. The illustration that I've used with all of them is "dead" Lake Erie. Everybody considers it "dead" until you tell them you're taking out of it 50 million pounds of fish a year. So you have a unique "dead" lake.

Once you can begin to find out that everything that you're reading isn't true, and you begin to say, "Let's take a look at both sides," there's a purpose.

My question is: What would you suggest that might enable us to direct something towards a specific program or a problem requiring the intelligence of a variety of attitudes and people towards its solution?

Can we, instead of proposing the books that have the answers, develop the books with the questions that have yet to be answered so we have a challenge for people?

DR. SHERRIFFS: What you are saying is so right. And what you're saying also is that we need frontiers, which in fact we are loaded with, if we'd only notice them. The frontiers didn't disappear when we hit the Pacific Ocean and stopped cutting down trees to put in cabins. The problem today is that the frontiers are more ideological and in the hands of the professors, and that's giving us some problems.

I'd like to mention something about my colleagues, present company very much excepted. There was a period when, with the population explosion and the resulting growth of the campus, we were adding, and I refer to this in my paper, a third to our faculty each year. Well, in four years, you've more than done in the old faculty in terms of numbers of youth. The original faculty members are retiring, dying, and so on.

The young came on the campus at a time when our society had placed intellect on a pedestal, when Sputnik was circling the earth and our society suddenly discovered science as one of those frontiers. When that happened, you'll recall, we went all-out to compete with Russia in scientific achievement.

We added to our faculties at a tremendous rate those young people who themselves had been very much pampered, babied, and rewarded as brightest in their classes. They served as valedictorians, were offered scholarships and fellowships and then were competed for by different colleges, which offered them a variety of inducements. The inducements included a reduced teaching load, so that those youthful brains could work on pushing forward the frontiers of knowledge.

Now the occupation I come from, which has as its union card the Ph.D., has also an occupational hazard: For a few minutes in history each one of us knows more about some specific area than does any other human being. It may be about blight in the Irish potato. It may be about cancer of some kind. But ours is a unique bit of individual research.

Very heady stuff, to think you know more about something than any other human being. It's heady stuff to have that happen to you on top of having been teacher's pet since you got around to education, to get those phenomenal wages you never heard about, and to get this very light teaching load, and now Harvard, Yale, and U.C.–Berkeley are competing for you. And then on your new campus you find out that there are lots of you. In fact, you outnumber the old guard that wrestled for and got tenure, that by responsible behavior was given academic freedom, and that, because it produced truly great teaching institutions, as well as research institutions, was allowed to appoint and promote its own folk. The old guard did that.

But you come in. The older faculty members have some humility. You don't yet, and you outnumber them. And it's from this new crowd, by and large, that we get these oversimplified approaches to life. They don't go through any initiation rites. They suddenly "own" the place, and the older people don't say, loudly enough, "There, there, you're going to risk these things we worked so hard to get. If you're going to use this institution, remember it has one fundamental value, above all—to pursue the truth wherever it leads, and not to pursue your bias wherever it leads."

But the old faculty's cautions were not heard because of a new creed: "My bias is moral and is more important than all that other stuff put together."

Now, most students fortunately are not sold by the pseudo-morality, or the excitement or the rhetoric of young faculty members who are pursuing their own biases, and acknowledgedly so, at the expense of a culture. And I think this is where the problem you're talking about lies. The faculty must take a responsible role. The silent members should say to their colleagues, "Knock it off." All must see that the burning of a Berkeley library means something much more than the loss of books. And the destruction of a scholar's papers, representing 12 years of work, is similarly ominous.

You talk to refugees from Europe about what it means, and they'll tell you mighty fast. More and more are speaking up and saying in essence, "I never dreamed in one life on this earth I might have to go through this twice." These behaviors, his shutting off any point of view but mine, because "mine is moral," and this bullying, violent, aggressive attack on people and on institutions, without conscience, because "I'm moral and you aren't," is something that we haven't really experienced here.

And the refugees will tell you that it was youth living in contempt of adult values who put Hitler in, not Hitler who took over and then found youth. I didn't understand that until some refugees shaped me up.

Now this is the worry: Will the faculty find its own code of ethics again? Will the faculty learn to preserve the most precious things that it can possibly contribute to this society?

I don't know. It had better.

JAMES GALLAGHER, Office of Education: I've heard the diagnosis but I don't think I've heard the therapy and I wonder if you'd like to address yourselves to it. If our institutions are weakened, how can they be strengthened specifically? If parents are unsure of what it is they should believe in, how do we make them more sure? And is the educational institution going to take the major responsibility for the moral upbringing of students instead of the church? That would be a change in the traditional way of doing things.

I'd like to hear some specifics in terms of just exactly

what you hope to do about institutions of higher education, or institutions of education in general, in order to strengthen those institutions, in order to strengthen parents and in order to make the educational system the center of moral preaching rather than the church.

DR. CLARK: It's obvious to me, and I'm sure that in stating your question you accept the fact, that there are no instant answers. There is no magic. We are dealing with a complexity of problems.

Human intelligence must be brought to bear. We have models of our society mobilizing its intellectual, its material, and its economic resources to seek answers and solutions to complex problems when it has committed itself to seek the answers and solutions.

In the lifetime of the present campus generation we have two major examples of the tremendous capacity of this society to solve the types of problems which it believes important enough to solve. The first has been in the area of the release of energy from matter, the atom. This was a major intellectual and engineering feat. It established a model of a type of social concern which was not widespread—a model of a great decision-making, policymaking commitment and resource allocation process. We used precisely that same model in dealing with the problem of space exploration when our collective national ego was jolted by Sputnik. You recall that the nation and the top policymakers of this nation decided that the American ego was going to be reestablished.

Dr. Sherriffs mentioned John Kennedy. One of the fascinating things in John Kennedy's brief administration was that he articulated the national commitment and goal to successful space exploration. In fact, he even stated the target date for the landing of an American on the moon.

I don't write those things off. To me, they are very important indications that when a society with the resources of our American society—which probably are greater than the resources of any other nation in history—makes up its mind to do something, even when it's foolish, it can do it. I don't believe that this is true only for things which seem to me to be not particularly important. I presume that there is some importance to getting material from the moon, and geologists must be learning a great deal and having their own particular type of academic ego-involvement with intellectual problems.

I believe that these models can be used as ways in which a democratic society can address itself to a rational, intelligent, moral restructuring of institutions so that those institutions become positively supportive of the perpetuation of all of the values which we here profess to have. But I believe we are not going to do it if we don't believe that it should be done or if biases and resistances of various sorts interfere, if we make them a part of the prejudices of the past.

It is interesting that we did not really have a popular referendum or public opinion poll on whether we should seek to release energy from matter or explore space. We didn't permit these kinds of issues to become matters of national debate and controversy until after we had acted on them.

That is not addressing myself directly to your question in

terms of my saying to you that I have the answers. It's addressing myself to your question only in terms of saying to you that we have the process by which we could get answers without the risk of chaos and random hostility and barbarity.

DR. SHERRIFFS: Clearly, in answer to your question, Mr. Gallagher, the cure, or the therapy, has to relate to the diagnosis. If the diagnosis is wrong, the therapies may be right, but only by chance. So within the position of my own diagnosis I'll react to your question.

In my own diagnosis, one of the reasons that a previously highly viable democratic society has been staggering is that its members have had so little of the information they need to make their own decisions—whether it's about their own young, whether it's about some of their institutions, or whatever.

So one of the first things I would say is: The more reliable the reporting of what goes on in the world around us by public officials, by news media, by college administrators, the sooner will the public be able to function effectively and without undue emotion in relation to its problems.

I think that to forget that the old math got us to the moon is all right, except that to become so awed by the new math that you can't help your kid with homework is to see it out of perspective. And this has a little cost; you keep adding up these little costs, and soon you've got a problem.

To refer constantly to such things as rolling a firebomb between the legs of a highway patrolman, incapacitating him for the rest of his life, as a "demonstration," produces a subtle kind of miseducation of the public. To talk about this as a "protest" about a specific public issue, rather than as sick behavior of an individual, is to confuse people even more. And a countervoice is so seldom heard.

I believe that members of boards and commissions, and administrators—whether boards of regents, or trustees, or presidents or chancellors of campuses—have got to be able to wear the two hats I have described, despite the difficulty of wearing them. Does this mean that we are going to have to have training, as we do in public administration, for public administration of public institutions? I don't know for sure, but these people must be free to respond to the public interest as well as to the faculty's needs. And they must understand the faculty's legitimate needs or they aren't really responding to the public interest.

As to whether it's a new profession we're talking about or better selection, different people have different ideas, but to me it's part of the problem.

The support of the responsible, scared faculty members by administrators who are now on the campuses would be a great help.

I brought with me, for example, grade sheets of 500 students in a row—all of them As, because the faculty members were afraid to give other grades. But if the administrators would lead, would get the faculty members together to talk to one another and find their own strengths and their own voices, much of what we're talking about could be worked on, I think, within the institution and not need to be effected from without.

A person who had high responsibility on one of our

greatest campuses recently asked me for a letter of recommendation for another position. I said, "Probably, but I'd like to ask you one question first: How much of your time did you spend with the run-of-the-mill students, or whatever you want to call them, on that campus?" His role was vice president of student affairs.

He said, "I'd rather not answer your question." And I said, "You asked for the letter." He said, "All right—about two hours a week." And I asked, "What were you doing the rest of the time?" He replied, "Seeing these other guys so we wouldn't have a confrontation, what do you think?"

Well, if you neglect those youngsters, who, depending on the campus, are 99 percent to 89 percent of the students, they will thus see no recourse, and they will see that one can get into an office fast, if one's ways of dealing with "the system" are against it or around it.

I think our youngsters deserve better than administrators who care only about the squeaky wheels. I think our society deserves better. I think, in fact, our faculty deserves better.

Obviously, now that we're where we are, safety has to be provided for students and faculty members who are afraid —in some cases, safety even at their homes.

When a faculty member or a student wakes up to find a firebomb in his bedroom, he doesn't speak out as quickly the next day as he might otherwise do. So there has to be—not as a solution to the long-run problem, but to make the long-run solution possible—sufficient protection of the unpopular, intimidated majority.

I think students are surprisingly unaware of what normal 17-to-23-year-olds are like. As a matter of fact, high school students are remarkably unaware of what that age group is like. If one talks to a high school audience about the need of an individual to work out his relation to his dependence and to his independence—and if one declares that a mature person is both dependent and independent—the students are grateful. If you explain that dependence is one reason why you marry and one reason why you care about children—you depend on them—the students are interested. And the students are pleased when you ask them, on the other hand, what is the use of their being, of their existing, if they aren't independent enough to be individuals.

Youngsters don't hear such things very often. "Independence is great, dependence is bad." Baloney. It's how much and of what kind you have of either.

Girls think too often that if they're virgins there's something wrong with them, enough so that it's the "in" thing, nowadays, to pretend to your roommate that you do things on dates that you really don't do. This was found in three major surveys on sex behavior. Adolescent males have long included those who talk about what they do on dates. When I went to Stanford I discovered—and it took me years to do so—that the guys who did all the talking, and were destroying the reputations of some girls, were the guys who did nothing. It was the silent ones the girls had to watch, you know!

Now the girls, research tells us, are doing what the boys once did, and yet their fundamental sex behavior hasn't changed, not statistically significantly, in decades. But the girls are not aware even in this area.

I believe it would be a very welcome relief just to make available to youth a nonpolitical description of a human being, without indoctrinating, without propagandizing, and without distorting.

I believe that society can't solve the educational crisis by law enforcement alone. It's got to be town and gown working together. It won't work otherwise.

The academic life expectancy of a typical student on the campus is about 2.4 years, as you no doubt know. You obviously can't solve the university's problem by educating just the student body. The students are gone by the time they've got the message.

You can work with faculty, however. You can work with administrators. But the best way is through organizations like this one, like the American Enterprise Institute, which can get the message to the educators while they still have their libraries.

Now, right or wrong, I suggest these things as therapy, and I granted you at the outset that the therapy relates to the correctness of the diagnosis. They're not easy solutions; they may work soon enough and they may not. But surely a simple autocratic response isn't going to do the job.

EARL H. JONES, District of Columbia Association of Classroom Teachers: I am somewhat concerned about the teacher's role. Today teachers have a pretty difficult time relating to the students, not only in your colleges and universities but in your elementary schools.

Therefore, my question is: What do you see the teacher doing in terms of achieving the relevant education? Is it going to be necessary to retrain these people or will the present-day teachers be able to do the job that is needed badly?

That question, by the way, I ask both you gentlemen, Dr. Clark and Dr. Sherriffs. Whichever one of you chooses to answer first is okay.

DR. CLARK: That's the type of question for which I think there's only one answer. Obviously, in any educational process, the teacher is the critical factor. The teacher's role is probably most important of all. Almost always, when I'm talking about the need for the serious reorganization of our educational system, I generally put most of my emphasis upon the elementary and secondary levels. I do this because I think the problems of higher education derive from the fundamental problems at the elementary and secondary levels. In all of my discussion of this problem and in the things that I've written about it, I generally get a feedback from teachers and teachers' groups indicating that their interpretation of what I say is critical and negative toward them.

Each time it happens, I am sort of surprised and disturbed and fascinated. Teachers are critically important. What I'm saying is that there's not going to be any major reform or increased relevance or significant reduction of anxiety in our educational system until the teaching profession—and here again I would say it is much more important on the elementary and secondary levels than on the higher educational level—develops the techniques, the methods, the form, the structure whereby it is enabled to function at that high level of efficiency it must have in order to give our young people the intellectual and moral equipment to cope with an increasingly complex and ambiguous society. Then all the other things we say about how to make education relevant will be irrelevant.

All this really means reform, in many dimensions, in the field of preparing teachers. It means that teacher-training institutions will have to be less idiotic than they have been, I think, in terms of their criteria of what it means to train teachers.

I use the word idiotic deliberately. I think it is idiotic to believe that one is training teachers in terms of a cafeteria-methodological-course approach to the problem when there's no evidence that methodology really equips the individual to deal with the complexities of things.

And when I look, as a member of the Board of Regents of New York State, at the requirements for teacher certification, and when I see what are considered to be the requirements for dealing with the awesome complexity of the human being, I really shudder. And I wonder how anybody comes out of that mumbo-jumbo, how any teacher, anyone who goes through a teacher-training institution, could come through with any sense of what it means.

I suspect that what has to happen is that most good teachers have to forget the nonsense that teacher-training institutions believe to be relevant.

I do think that any overall system of educational reform

will not only have to address itself to the preparation of new teachers as the number one item on the agenda, but will also have to address itself to a very effective and serious and practical program for the education, the reeducation of present teachers. Such a program would have to devote itself to planning realistic ways of motivating individuals in the teaching profession—ways not unlike the ways in which other professions are motivated in order to put a floor on the level of performance.

In our society—whether our young people like it or not, and I suppose many of them will not question this—one of the most effective ways of motivating individuals for high-level performance in a profession is through differential remuneration. It seems to me that the teaching profession has suffered, and is well on its way towards a deadening kind of stagnation in mediocrity, because it has not faced realistically this consideration: Given the limitations of human beings, given the fact that human beings are not yet angels, productivity and performance, to be motivated for a level beyond the minimal, must have differential rewards. There must be some relationship between reward and level of performance. I think this is a very important point.

DR. SHERRIFFS: I'm glad you said what you said, Dr. Clark, because I feel that much of what I would have said you have covered very well.

I, too, think that teaching is probably the most important profession which relates to the age levels we're discussing, and I think that motivation is the most important variable within teaching.

Most of the studies I know of, on size of class, on color of chalk, on almost anything you can think of, are equivocal in results, except that a well-motivated teacher with a large class does a much better job than an unmotivated teacher with a little class, and so on. But if we've got somebody who comes alive, if the selection process itself gets the people who would respond with delight in seeing people grow, curiosity develop, and the rest of it, we'll succeed.

I think the merit system, which is what I think you're talking to, Dr. Clark, and you didn't use the word tenure, I noticed, but——

DR. CLARK: No, I didn't use those words.

DR. SHERRIFFS: ——it's a risky one to use at this hour of the day, but either tenure plus merit or a reevaluation of tenure itself is past due.

As we all know, thinking back in our own lives, the teachers that really loved getting us to discover the value of learning were the ones that made it for us—whether they used lots of books on the reading list or few, and whether they were strict or permissive was much less important. It was whether they shared the thrill we felt. To get back to that is what we must do, and I think the things you were suggesting will get us there, Dr. Clark.

The American Enterprise Institute for Public Policy Research was created in 1943 as a unique, nonprofit and nonpartisan research and educational organization. AEI's purpose is to assist the nation's policymakers, legislators, and educational leaders by providing them —and making available to the public— factual analyses and studies of important current issues.

Recognition of the growing importance of academic influence on national policy came from President Johnson during an address at Princeton University in May 1966, when he said:

> In almost every field of governmental concern, from economics to national security, the academic community has become a central instrument of public policy in these United States.

AEI has tapped this rich resource of brainpower for the past 25 years. From a roster of the nation's leading scholars, it selects experts to conduct research and study projects on the many public policy problems confronting the nation. Besides its Rational Debate Series, AEI also publishes Long-Range Studies on major public policy issues and a Legislative Analysis Series which outlines the pros and cons of major bills and issues before Congress.

Informed policymakers are vital to the maintenance of national policies which promote rather than impede a strong nation and a dynamic market economy. The growing volume and complexity of basic policy proposals to be decided each year makes most difficult the task of the sincere legislator, administrator, and thinking citizen to understand clearly the total significance and implication of each major policy decision.